# FRANCHISING IN CHINA 2014

## *Legal and Business Considerations*

AF873380

KENDAL H. TYRE, JR., EXECUTIVE EDITOR
DIANA VILMENAY-HAMMOND, MANAGING EDITOR
PIERCE HAESUNG HAN, ASSISTANT EDITOR

LEXNOIR FOUNDATION

FOURTH QUARTER 2014

LexNoir Foundation is the charitable, educational arm of LexNoir, an international network of lawyers connecting the African Diaspora.



www.lexnoir.org

Table of Contents

Page

## ***Bibliography of International Franchise Resources***

Kendal H. Tyre, Jr., Diana Vilmenay-Hammond, Pierce Haesung Han and Keri McWilliams
NIXON PEABODY LLP

# Acknowledgment

This book could not have been written without the hard work and dedication of each of the contributing authors and editors. Thank you.

We would like to acknowledge and extend our heartfelt gratitude to Maria Stallings of the Washington, D.C. office of Nixon Peabody LLP for her invaluable assistance in revising, proofing, and editing this publication.

# About the Editors and Authors

**Kendal H. Tyre, Jr.** – Kendal is a partner in the Washington, D.C. office of Nixon Peabody LLP. He handles domestic and cross-border transactions, including mergers and acquisitions, joint ventures, strategic alliances, licensing, and franchise matters.

In his franchise and licensing practice, Kendal counsels domestic and international franchisors, franchisees, licensors, licensees and distributors regarding U.S. state and federal franchise laws as well as foreign franchise legislation in a variety of jurisdictions. Kendal drafts and provides advice with regard to franchise and license agreements, disclosure documents and area development agreements and has extensive experience drafting and negotiating a variety of other commercial agreements. His client base spans the United States and foreign countries, including South Africa, Kenya, and the United Kingdom.

Kendal is a frequent contributor to franchise publications and a frequent speaker at franchise programs held by the American Bar Association Forum on Franchising and the International Franchise Association.

Kendal is co-chair of the firm's Diversity Action Committee and its Africa Group. Kendal is also the executive director of LexNoir Foundation.

E-mail address: ktyre@nixonpeabody.com

**Diana Vilmenay-Hammond** – Diana is an attorney in the Washington, D.C. office of Nixon Peabody LLP. She is a member of the firm's Franchise & Distribution team.

In her franchise practice, Diana works with domestic and international franchisors on transactional and litigation matters. Specifically, she counsels franchisor clients regarding state and federal franchise laws, disclosure and registration obligations. Diana drafts and negotiates various commercial agreements, including international franchise and development agreements.

Diana has co-authored numerous articles on franchising and frequently co-hosted the Nixon Peabody franchise law webinar series. Topics have included:

- "Franchise Case Law Round-Up: Implications for Your Franchise;"
- "Social Media Part II: Best Practices in Protecting Your Brand in the New Media;" and
- "The Awuah Case: Bellwether or Outlier."

Diana received her J.D. from Howard University School of Law and her B.A. from Georgetown University. She is a member of the American Bar Association (Forum on Franchising).

E-mail address: dvilmenay@nixonpeabody.com

**Pierce Haesung Han** – Pierce is an associate in Nixon Peabody's Global Business & Transactions group. Pierce focuses his practice on three main areas, assisting clients with a variety of complex business transactions.

- Mergers & Acquisitions: Providing assistance to both public and private clients with various mergers and acquisitions, performing due diligence, drafting and negotiating transaction documents, and facilitating closing and post-closing mechanics.
- International Commercial Transactions: Drafting and negotiating a variety of commercial agreements,

including international franchise and development agreements, license agreements, and purchase and sale agreements.

- Federal Securities Law Matters: Assisting public and private clients regarding federal securities laws and stock exchange rules relating to corporate governance and disclosure.

Pierce received his J.D. from Georgetown University Law Center and his B.A. from Case Western Reserve University. He is admitted to practice in the State of New York and the District of Columbia.

E-mail address: phan@nixonpeabody.com

**Keri McWilliams** – Keri is an associate in the Franchise & Distribution team of Nixon Peabody LLP. Keri works with clients on a number of franchising issues, including obtaining and maintaining franchise registrations in various states, responding to state inquiries regarding trade practices, ongoing compliance with state and federal regulations, and updating franchise disclosure documents. She also handles franchise sales counseling and franchise system issues.

Keri is a member of the American Bar Association's Forum on Franchising, and the Federal and Minnesota State bar associations. She is also a member of Minnesota Women Lawyers and the Minnesota Association of Black Lawyers, and a volunteer in the Volunteer Lawyers Network.

Keri received her J.D. from Georgetown University Law Center and her B.F.A. from Washington University. She is admitted to practice in the District of Columbia and Minnesota.

E-mail address: kmcwilliams@nixonpeabody.com

**David K. Cheng** – David Cheng is the chair and managing partner of Nixon Peabody's China and Asia-Pacific practice. He is qualified in both the United States and Hong Kong. He focuses on cross-border transactions, litigations and investigations, advising on issues ranging from acquisitions, capital financing (initial public offering), intellectual property protection and disputes to fraud, FCPA and SEC investigations. He has a client portfolio from all over the world: United States, Middle East, Europe, Japan, Singapore, Taiwan, China and Hong Kong.

David received his J.D. from Golden Gate University School of Law, LL.M. from Georgetown University Law Center and his B.A. and B.S. from University of California, Davis. He is admitted to practice in California, the District of Columbia, the U.S. Tax Court, the U.S. Supreme Court and Hong Kong.

E-mail address: dcheng@nixonpeabody.com

**Kelly F. Xiang** – Kelly Xiang focuses her practice on cross-border matters involving China, including all forms of foreign direct investments in China, market entries, mergers and acquisitions, commercial franchising, labor and employment, immigration, taxes, licensing, regulatory issues, general corporate matters and IP-related matters including trademark, branding and licensing.

Kelly received her M.Phil, in Law, from the University of Hong Kong and her M.A., B.A. from Peking University. She also completed a Postgraduate Program in Law at the University of Macau. She is admitted to practice in the People's Republic of China.

E-mail address: kxiang@nixonpeabody.com

# About the Book

*Franchising in China 2014: Legal and Business Considerations* contains excerpts from the larger work *Franchising in Asia 2014: Legal and Business Considerations*. Both books serve as practical, succinct, easy-to-use reference tools for lawyers, business people and academics to use in navigating the laws and business issues impacting franchise arrangements in Asia.

This book provides an overview of the franchise industry in China and addresses the typical legal issues confronted when expanding a franchise system in China. The larger work, *Franchising in Asia 2014: Legal and Business Considerations*, covers those laws governing franchising in several other Asian countries.

In both books, an author, who is a legal expert in the designated jurisdiction, addresses the basic questions that a franchise lawyer would need to know to competently represent a client in expanding their franchise system to that country.

Each country chapter organizes a discussion of that country's laws under various headings and in a uniform format. Topics were sent to each country's author in the form of a questionnaire, and each author drafted responses to the questions presented. A general overview relating to the political and economic history of the country at the beginning of each chapter provides an initial context for the regulatory framework.[1]

---

1 The source of information for these sections is the Central Intelligence Agency, https://www.cia.gov/library/publications/the-world-factbook/ (last visited June 29, 2014).

Apart from an overview of the legal framework for franchising, each book contains other articles and resources that should prove useful to those in the franchise industry.

The authors for each chapter are listed at the beginning of a chapter and their biographical information is listed in the previous section, *About the Editors and Authors*.

Readers should always consult with local counsel in the relevant jurisdiction instead of relying solely on the information contained in this book. The laws governing franchising are evolving and local counsel in China are best positioned to provide timely, relevant advice applying the current law to the particular facts of a case.

# Franchising in China

*David K. Cheng and Kelly F. Xiang*
*NIXON PEABODY LLP*
**Shanghai, China**

# China

## I. Introduction

### A. Historical Background of the Country

After World War II, the communists under Mao Zedong established an autocratic socialist system that, while ensuring China's sovereignty, imposed strict controls over everyday life. After 1978, Mao's successor Deng Xiaoping and other leaders focused on market-oriented economic development and by 2000 output had quadrupled. For much of the population, living standards have improved dramatically and the room for personal choice has expanded, yet political controls remain tight. Since the early 1990s, China has increased its global outreach and participation in international organizations.

### B. Economy of the Country

Since the late 1970s China has moved from a closed, centrally planned system to a more market-oriented one that plays a major global role. In 2010, China became the world's largest exporter. Reforms began with the phasing out of collectivized agriculture, and expanded to include the gradual liberalization of prices, fiscal decentralization, increased autonomy for state enterprises, growth of the private sector, development of stock markets and a modern banking system, and opening to foreign trade and investment. China has implemented reforms in a gradualist fashion.

In recent years, China has renewed its support for state-owned enterprises in sectors considered important to "economic security," explicitly looking to foster globally competitive industries. After keeping its currency tightly linked to the U.S. dollar for years, in July 2005, China moved to an exchange rate system that references a basket of currencies. From mid-2005 to late 2008, cumulative appreciation of the renminbi against the U.S. dollar was more than 20%, but the exchange rate remained virtually pegged to the dollar from the onset of the global financial crisis until June 2010, when Beijing allowed resumption of a gradual appreciation and expanded the daily trading band within which the RMB is permitted to fluctuate. The restructuring of the economy and resulting efficiency gains have contributed to a more than tenfold increase in GDP since 1978. Measured on a purchasing power parity (PPP) basis that adjusts for price differences, China in 2013 stood as the second-largest economy in the world after the US, having surpassed Japan in 2001. The dollar values of China's agricultural and industrial output each exceed those of the U.S.; China is second to the U.S. in the value of services it produces. Still, per capita income is below the world average.

The Chinese government faces numerous economic challenges, including: (a) reducing its high domestic savings rate and correspondingly low domestic consumption; (b) facilitating higher-wage job opportunities for the aspiring middle class, including rural migrants and increasing numbers of college graduates; (c) reducing corruption and other economic crimes; and (d) containing environmental damage and social strife related to the economy's rapid transformation.

Economic development has progressed further in coastal provinces than in the interior, and by 2011 more than 250 million migrant workers and their dependents had relocated to urban areas to find work. One consequence of population control policy is that China is now one of the most rapidly aging countries in the world. Deterioration in the environment (notably air pollution, soil erosion, and the steady fall of the water table, especially in the North) is another long-term problem. China continues to lose arable land because of erosion and economic development. The

Chinese government is seeking to add energy production capacity from sources other than coal and oil, focusing on nuclear and alternative energy development. Several factors are converging to slow China's growth, including debt overhang from its credit-fueled stimulus program, industrial overcapacity, inefficient allocation of capital by state-owned banks, and the slow recovery of China's trading partners.

The government's 12th Five-Year Plan, adopted in March 2011 and reiterated at the Communist Party's "Third Plenum" meeting in November 2013, emphasizes continued economic reforms and the need to increase domestic consumption in order to make the economy less dependent in the future on fixed investments, exports, and heavy industry. However, China has made only marginal progress toward these rebalancing goals. The new government of President Xi Jinping has signaled a greater willingness to undertake reforms that focus on China's long-term economic health, including giving the market a more decisive role in allocating resources.

### C. Franchise Legal Overview

In China, franchise transactions are regulated specifically by the Regulations on the Administration of Commercial Franchise – February 2007; (the "2007 Regulations") Administrative Measures for Archival Filing of Commercial Franchises – December 2011(the "Archival Filing Measures"); and the Administration Measures for the Information Disclosure of Commercial Franchises – February 2012 (the "Disclosure Measures"). The applicable laws do not provide for any exclusions, exceptions, or exemptions.

## II. Regulatory Requirements

### A. Pre-sale Disclosure

*Please describe any pre-sale franchise disclosure or similar requirements that may apply to franchise transactions.*

The 2007 Regulations and the Disclosure Measures mandate prior disclosure before the signing of the franchise agreement.

A franchisor in China is required to provide a franchisee with accurate information on specified matters concerning the franchise system and the proposed franchise contract at least 30 days before the franchise contract is executed, except in those instances when the franchisor and the franchisee are renewing a contract on terms identical to that of their existing franchise contract. However, the 2007 Regulations and the Disclosure Measures are silent on whether disclosure is required on the transfer of a franchise.

There are no specific provisions in the 2007 Regulations that apply to letters of intent related to any part of a franchise business transaction. According to the 2007 Regulations, if a franchisor requires a franchisee to pay expenses before conclusion of the franchising contract, the franchisor shall explain in written form to the franchisee about the application of these expenses and the conditions and methods for the refund of these expenses.

In addition, the franchisor is required to inform the franchisee promptly of any significant change in the information provided in the disclosure document.

### B. Government Approvals, Registrations, Filing Requirements

*Please describe any necessary government approvals, registrations, or filing requirements that may apply to franchise transactions.*

Under the 2007 Regulations, a franchisor must be an enterprise, but it does not require that the franchisor be an enterprise incorporated in China. In order to become a franchisor, the enterprise must have a mature operation method and the ability to provide continuous guidance, technical support and business training to the franchisee. The enterprise must own at least two stores that it operates directly and have been in operation for more than one year ("Qualification and 2+1 Rule").

Within 15 days of the execution of the franchise agreement, the franchisor is required to file with the Ministry of Commerce ("MOFCOM") or its local counterpart at the provincial level:

1. Copy of its incorporation certificate or business license;
2. Standard form of its franchise agreement;
3. Franchise operation manual;
4. Marketing plan;
5. Written commitment to meet the requirements of Qualification and 2+1 Rule and related supporting documents; and
6. If the product or service under the franchise requires special approval, the related approval documents.

If the franchisor engages in franchising within one province, it must file the above documents with MOFCOM's local counterpart at the provincial level; if the franchisor engages in franchising in more than one province, it shall file those documents with MOFCOM, but in practice, MOFCOM normally authorizes its local counterpart at provincial level to handle this matter. A foreign franchisor engaging in cross-border franchising in China must file those documents with MOFCOM.

### C. Limits on Fees and Typical Term of Franchise Agreement

*Please describe any limits upon the nature and extent of fees and the term of a typical franchise agreement.*

The parties may freely agree on the nature, amount or payment of fees. Initial fees and royalties are common in China. The franchise term specified in the franchise agreement shall not be less than three years, unless the franchisee agrees otherwise. This provision shall not apply when the franchisor and franchisee renew the franchise agreement.

## III. Currency

*If all payments under a franchise agreement must be made in immediately available U.S. Dollars, please advise as to any restrictions, reporting requirements, or regulations concerning the exchange, repatriation or remittance of U.S. Dollars.*

At present, China maintains general foreign exchange control and RMB is not freely convertible. Payment of fees to a foreign franchisor is deemed as current account transactions under Chinese law. The parties may freely agree on the nature, amount or payment of fees. For payments for trade in services, when a single receipt or payment is over US $50,000, the applicant shall submit transaction documents to the bank for its review, for example, for royalties for use of proprietary rights and franchise fees, the applicant shall submit relevant contract (agreement) and invoice (payment notice) to the bank for its review.

## IV. Taxes, Tariffs, and Duties

*Please do not provide any in-depth comments on tax structuring. However, please provide your general comments on the typical amount of withholding tax that would apply and whether a "gross-up" provision contained in a franchise agreement would be enforceable in your country.*

China has strict regulations and procedures regarding withholding tax from non-tax resident enterprises for their China-sourced income. In China, franchisees are required to withhold income tax on payments to a U.S. franchisor at a rate of 10%, subject to the double taxation treaty with the U.S. and value-added tax at a rate of 6%.

## V. Trademarks

*Please advise us as to whether there are any special requirements for granting a valid trademark license, including the use of a registered user agreement or a short trademark license agreement and any required filing of such an agreement with the trademark authorities.*

In China, the 2007 Regulations specify that the patent or trademark licenses related to the franchised operations are to be implemented according to the laws and administrative regulations on patent or trademarks. Given this, franchisors shall file the license agreement at the patent bureau or trademark office in the People's Republic of China.

## VI. Restrictions on Transfer

*Please advise as to whether there are any restrictions (1) on a franchisor to restrict transfers by a master franchisee, any interest in a master franchisee, or the assets of the master franchisee or (2) the ability of a master franchisee to control and/or restrict transfers of a subfranchisee's rights under a master franchise agreement, an interest in the subfranchisee, or the assets of the subfranchisee.*

Pursuant to 2007 Regulations, a franchisee may not assign its franchise rights to a third party without the consent of the franchisor.

## VII. Termination

*Please advise us as to any laws relating to termination in your country, such as agency laws, required indemnity provisions, notice or "good cause" requirements, or other laws affecting termination of a franchise agreement. Please describe.*

According to the 2007 Regulations, a franchisor and the franchisee shall specify in the franchising contract that the franchisee may unilaterally terminate the contract within a certain term after the conclusion of such franchising contract. In addition, if a franchisor conceals relevant information or provides false information to a franchisee, the franchisee can terminate the franchising contract. Other than the abovementioned provisions, there is no known special provision regarding termination of a franchise agreement.

## VIII. Governing Law, Jurisdiction, and Dispute Resolution

### A. Choice of Law of Foreign Jurisdiction

*Please confirm whether the choice of law of a foreign jurisdiction would likely to be upheld under the law of the country, except for certain matters such as trademarks, bankruptcy and competition matters, which we assume would be governed by the law in your country.*

There are no restrictions on the applicable governing law of the franchising contract with foreign elements, e.g., involving a foreign party.

### B. International Arbitration Dispute Resolution

*Please confirm that a court in your country would honor an election of international arbitration dispute resolution, and therefore refuse to hear any disputes arising under a franchise agreement.*

China is a signatory to the *Convention on the Recognition and Enforcement of Foreign Arbitral Awards* (the "New York Convention"). It is common for franchisors to require the parties engage in mediation or arbitration to resolve disputes.

## IX. Non-Competition Provisions

*If the franchise agreement prohibits the franchisee from engaging in certain competitive activities during the term of the agreement, and for a 12-month period after the termination or expiration of the agreement, please comment on the enforceability of non-competition covenants in your country.*

Generally, in China, there are no legal restrictions on non-compete clauses so long as they are reasonable.

## X. Language Requirements

*Does the law in your country require that a franchise agreement be translated into the local language in order to be enforceable between the parties?*

There is no mandatory requirement to use Chinese in contracting, so English is an acceptable language. However, in any court proceedings in China, the court requires Chinese translations of all documents, whether pleadings or documentary evidence. Also, for governmental filing purposes, the Chinese governmental agencies normally require a Chinese version of any document to be filed. In addition, banks normally require a Chinese translation of the supporting documents (e.g., franchise agreement) to transfer royalties outside China. Normally, the Chinese translation should be provided by a Chinese licensed translation company.

## XI. Other Significant Matters

*Please advise as to whether there are any significant matters not addressed above of which a franchisor should be aware in connection with its entering into a franchise agreement in your country.*

Each year by March 31, a franchisor shall report to the record filing authority information on its entry into, and rescission, termination and renewal of, franchisee contracts during the preceding year.

China Franchising Association is the local franchise association in China. There is no legal requirement that a franchisor must become a member of such association.

# Bibliography of International Franchise Resources

*Kendal H. Tyre, Jr., Diana Vilmenay-Hammond, Pierce Haesung Han and Keri McWilliams*
*Nixon Peabody LLP*
**Washington, D.C.**

## I. General International Resources

Mark Abell, Gary R. Duvall, and Andrea Oricchio Kirsh, *International Franchise Legislation* B1, ABA FORUM ON FRANCHISING (1996)

Kathleen C. Anderson and Anthony M. Stiegler, *Put Muscle in Your Marks: Enforcing Intellectual Property Rights* W14, ABA FORUM ON FRANCHISING (1995)

Richard M. Asbill and Jane W. LaFranchi, *International Franchise Sales Laws—A Survey* W7, ABA FORUM ON FRANCHISING (2005)

Jeffery A. Brimer, Alison C. McElroy, and John Pratt, *Going International: What Additional Restraints Will You Face?* W4, ABA FORUM ON FRANCHISING (2011)

Michael G. Brennan, Alexander Konigsberg, and Philip F. Zeidman, *Globetrotting: A Workshop on International Franchising* 10/W8, ABA FORUM ON FRANCHISING (1994)

Michael G. Brennan, Alexander Konigsberg, and Philip F. Zeidman, *Globetrotting: Strategies for Launching U.S.*

*Franchisors Abroad* 2/P2, ABA FORUM ON FRANCHISING (1994)

Christopher P. Bussert and Jennifer Dolman, *Regaining Your Trademark After Abandonment or Misappropriation* W7, ABA FORUM ON FRANCHISING (2011)

Ronald T. Coleman and Linda K. Stevens, *Trade Secrets and Confidential Information: Rights and Remedies* W2, ABA FORUM ON FRANCHISING (2000)

Finola Cunningham, *Commerce Department Helps Franchisors Go Global*, in FRANCHISING WORLD 63 (Dec. 2005)

Michael R. Daigle and Alex S. Konigsberg, *Meeting Off-Shore Disclosure and Contract Requirements* F/W13, ABA FORUM ON FRANCHISING (1992)

Jennifer Dolman, Robert A. Lauer, and Lawrence M. Weinberg, Structuring International Master Franchise Relationships for Success and Responding When Things Go Awry W22, ABA FORUM ON FRANCHISING (2007)

Gary R. Duvall, Paul Jones, and Jane LaFranchi, *Planning for the International Enforcement of Franchise Agreements* W6, ABA FORUM ON FRANCHISING (1999)

William Edwards, International Expansion: Do Opportunities Outweigh Challenges? in FRANCHISING WORLD (February 2008)

George J. Eydt and Stuart Hershman, *Bringing a Foreign Franchise System to the United States* W9, ABA FORUM ON FRANCHISING (2009)

William A. Finkelstein and Louis T. Pirkey, *International Trademarks* W15, ABA FORUM ON FRANCHISING (1991)

William A. Finkelstein, Protecting Trademarks Internationally: Current Strategies and Developments B3, ABA FORUM ON FRANCHISING (1996)

Stephen Giles, Lou H. Jones, and Lawrence Weinberg, *Negotiating and Documenting Complex International Franchise Agreements* W21, ABA FORUM ON FRANCHISING (2006)

Steven M. Goldman, Stephen Giles, Marc Israel, and Stanley Wong, *Competition Round Up from Around the World* LB2, ABA FORUM ON FRANCHISING (2004)

David C. Gryce and E. Lynn Perry, *Trademarks and Copyrights in the International Arena* 6/W4, ABA FORUM ON FRANCHISING (1993)

Kenneth S. Kaplan, Andrew P. Loewinger, and Penelope J. Ward, *System Standards in International Franchising* W14, ABA FORUM ON FRANCHISING (2005)

Edward Levitt and Jorge Mondragon, A Survey of International Legal Traps and How to Avoid Them—Beyond the Franchise Laws W20, ABA FORUM ON FRANCHISING (2007)

Ned Levitt, Kendal H. Tyre, and Penny Ward, *The Impossible Dream: Controlling Your International Franchise System* W4, ABA FORUM ON FRANCHISING (2010)

Michael K. Lindsey and Andrew P. Loewinger, *International (Non-U.S.) Franchise Disclosure Requirements* W9, ABA FORUM ON FRANCHISING (2002)

Andrew P. Loewinger and John Pratt, *Recent Changes and Trends in International Franchise Laws* W4, ABA FORUM ON FRANCHISING (2008)

Andrew P. Loewinger and Thomas M. Pitegoff, Avoiding the Long Arm of the Law in International Franchising: Issues and Approaches W8, ABA FORUM ON FRANCHISING (1995)

Craig J. Madson and Katherine C. Spelman, *Similarity and Confusion in the Intellectual Property Arena* W11, ABA FORUM ON FRANCHISING (1997)

Christopher A. Nowak, John Pratt, and Carl E. Zwisler, *Franchising Internationally with Countries with Opaque Legal Systems* W20, ABA FORUM ON FRANCHISING (2006)

E. Lynn Perry and John L. Sullivan Jr., *Trademark Compliance and Enforcement Techniques* E/W12, ABA FORUM ON FRANCHISING (1992)

Marcel Portmann, *Franchising Sector Proves Global Reach,* in FRANCHISING WORLD (January 2007)

John Pratt and Luiz Henrique O. do Amaral, Civil Law for Common Law Practitioners (or How to Draft an Agreement for Use Overseas) W4, ABA FORUM ON FRANCHISING (2002)

Kirk W. Reilly, Robert F. Salkowski and Geoffrey B. Shaw, *Determining the Rules of Engagement in Litigation Here and Abroad* W5, ABA FORUM ON FRANCHISING (2008)

Catherine Riesterer and Frank Zaid, *Basics of International Franchising* L/B2, ABA FORUM ON FRANCHISING (1997)

W. Andrew Scott and Christopher N. Wormald, *Stranger in a Strange Land: Contrasting Franchising in International Expansion* W2, ABA FORUM ON FRANCHISING (2003)

Donald Smith and Erik Wulff, *International Franchising: The Unraveling of an International Franchise Relationship* 15/W13, ABA FORUM ON FRANCHISING (1993)

Frank Zaid, Pamela Mills, and Michael Santa Maria, *Essential Issues in International Franchising* LB/1, ABA FORUM ON FRANCHISING (2001)

## II. Asian Resources

Stephen Giles, Andrew P. Loewinger, and Sherin Sakr, *Go East Young Franchisor: Franchising in Asia-Pacific Other Than China and India* W21, ABA FORUM ON FRANCHISING (2011)

Stephen Giles, *Franchising in Asia-Pacific Region, Who's Who Legal*: FRANCHISE 2012 (2012)

### A. China

Ren Yanling, *Changes to Chinese Franchise Law: An improved Balance Between the Interests of Franchisors and Franchisees*, in INT'L JOURNAL OF FRANCHISING LAW 3 (2012)

*China: New Franchsing Law, in Int'l Journal of* FRANCHISING LAW 2 (2005)

Ella S.K. Cheong, *China*, in INTERNATIONAL FRANCHISING CHN/1 (Dennis Campbell gen. ed. 2011)

Yu Qin and Richard L. Wageman, *China*, in INTERNATIONAL FRANCHISE SALES LAWS China-1 (Andrew P. Loewinger and Michael K. Lindsey eds. 2010)

Mark Abell, Daniela C. Brito, and Paul D. Jones, *Franchising in the BRIC Markets (Brazil, Russia, India, and China)* W18, ABA FORUM ON FRANCHISING (2008)

### B. Hong Kong

Andrea S.Y. Fong, *Hong Kong*, in INTERNATIONAL FRANCHISING HK/1 (Dennis Campbell gen. ed. 2011)

### C. India

Preeti Mehta, *India—Termination of Master Franchise Agreements and the Consequences*, in INT'L JOURNAL OF FRANCHISING LAW 3 (2007)

Yoginder Pal, *Franchising in India*, FRANCHISING WORLD (October 2006)

Mark Abell, Daniela C. Brito and Paul D. Jones, *Franchising in the BRIC Markets (Brazil, Russia, India, and China)* W18, ABA FORUM ON FRANCHISING (2008)

### D. Indonesia

Sigit Ardianto and Rivan F. Ramadhan, *Indonesia*, in INTERNATIONAL FRANCHISING INA/1 (Dennis Campbell gen. ed. 2011)

Rick Beckman and Ferry P. Madian, *Indonesia*, in INTERNATIONAL FRANCHISE SALES LAWS Indonesia-1 (Andrew P. Loewinger and Michael K. Lindsey eds. 2010)

Kendal H. Tyre, Jr. & Pierce Haesung Han, *The Ministry of Trade of Indonesia Limits Growth of Food and Beverage*

*Franchises*, NIXON PEABODY LLP: FRANCHISE ALERT (February 2013)

### E. Japan

Takenari Shimizu, *Japan*, in INTERNATIONAL FRANCHISING JAP/1 (Dennis Campbell gen. ed. 2011)

Souichirou Kozuka and Takashi Kanai, *Japan*, in INTERNATIONAL FRANCHISE SALES LAWS Japan-1 (Andrew P. Loewinger and Michael K. Lindsey eds. 2010)

### F. Malaysia

Leela Baskaran, *Malaysia*, in INTERNATIONAL FRANCHISING MAY/1 (Dennis Campbell gen. ed. 2011)

Mohd Bustaman Hj Abdullah and Wong Sai Fong, *Malaysia*, in INTERNATIONAL FRANCHISE SALES LAWS Malaysia-1 (Andrew P. Loewinger and Michael K. Lindsey eds. 2010)

Kendal H. Tyre, Jr. & Pierce Haesung Han, *Malaysian Government Actively Promotes Growth in Franchise Sector*, NIXON PEABODY LLP: FRANCHISE ALERT (October 2013)

Kendal H. Tyre, Jr. & Pierce Haesung Han, *Tapping Into Malaysia's Aggressive Franchising Goals*, PORTFOLIO MEDIA, INC.: LAW360 (November 2013)

### G. Singapore

Daniel Lim, Bernard Lui, Michele The, and Vanessa Chew, *Singapore*, in INTERNATIONAL FRANCHISING SIN/1 (Dennis Campbell gen. ed. 2011)

### H. South Korea

Brendon Carr and Jae-Hoon Kim, *South Korea*, in INTERNATIONAL FRANCHISE SALES LAWS South Korea-1 (Andrew P. Loewinger and Michael K. Lindsey eds. 2010)

Kendal H. Tyre, Jr. & Pierce Haesung Han, *South Korea adopts major amendments to the Fair Transactions in Franchise Business Act*, NIXON PEABODY LLP: FRANCHISE LAW ALERT (January 2014)

### I. Taiwan

Wellington Liu and David Lu, *Taiwan*, in INTERNATIONAL FRANCHISE SALES LAWS Taiwan-1 (Andrew P. Loewinger and Michael K. Lindsey eds. 2010)

### J. Thailand

Alan Adcock and Sriwan Puapondh, *Thailand*, in INTERNATIONAL FRANCHISING THA/1 (Dennis Campbell gen. ed. 2011)

### K. Vietnam

Mai Minh Hang and Nguyen Anh Tran, *Vietnam*, in INTERNATIONAL FRANCHISE SALES LAWS Vietnam-1 (Andrew P. Loewinger and Michael K. Lindsey eds. 2010)

Printed in Dunstable, United Kingdom

91343673R00020